FABULOUS FALL FRENZY

by

Malinda Rowe

Illustrations by Faith Belt

Dedicated to my parents, Kenny and Lynn Rowe,
who encouraged imagination and innovation.

Text copyright © 2023 by Malinda Rowe
Illustrations copyright © 2023 by Faith Belt
Published by The Wordly Group
Printed in the U.S.A.
First Printing, 2023
ISBN: 978-1-7350221-4-7
The Wordly Group
www.thewordlygroup.com

FABULOUS FALL FRENZY

by

Malinda Rowe

Illustrations by Faith Belt

It's that time of year again. The leaves are turning beautiful colors.

Reds, yellows, and oranges.

Momma calls it my "fall frenzy."

I look for the most colorful and perfect leaves I can find.

My sister and brother want to jump in piles of them today.

I have some fun **ideas** too!

The first thing I do is stack some books on my leaves to *flatten* them out while they dry.

When they are nice and flat and dry, I take them from under the books.

That's when the *fun* begins.

I put paper on them and rub crayons over the paper to make my own fall picture.

I think I will make an art gallery.

Some of the leaves make
really nice feathers.

Momma gives me an old shoe box,
and I make a fairy house out of it.

The whole outside is covered with colorful leaves.

I save some of the leaves for
the fairy's bed and blanket.

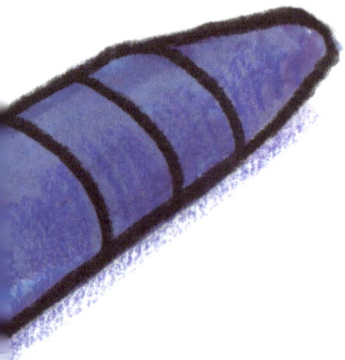

I hang some of my leaves from strings all around our house.

I decorate the table too.

Every house should be full of beautiful fall leaves!

When it's time to
trick or treat,
I'm going to dress
up as a pile of leaves.

I ask Momma if she has some glass
jars that I can decorate.

I cover them with *pretty* leaves, and
Momma uses them for candles.

Our yard is so full of leaves that I can rake out
a perfectly proper *little house* to play in.

I make a path to our house in case
Momma wants to come over for a visit.

I invite my sister and brother over to my
leaf house for some hot chocolate.

Daddy makes good hot chocolate.
He has hot chocolate with us.

It's almost our bedtime.
We need to make our leaf beds.

They smell sooooo good –
just like a perfect fall day!

I save a few of my pretty leaves
between the pages of a book.

When it is snowy and cold, I can remember all
of the fun I had while I wait for next fall.

By then, I will have lots of new ideas for my leaves!

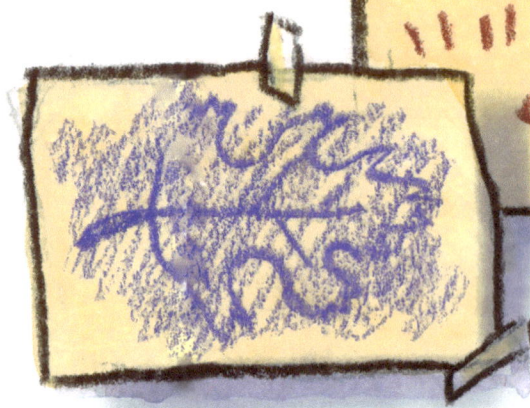

www.ingramcontent.com/pod-product-compliance
Lightning Source LLC
Chambersburg PA
CBHW042106090426

42811CB00018B/1866